DISCOVER
DRAGONS
DO YOU BELIEVE?

This series features creatures that excite our minds. They're magic. They're myth. They're mystery. They're also not real. They live in our stories.

45TH PARALLEL PRESS

Published in the United States of America by Cherry Lake Publishing Group
Ann Arbor, Michigan
www.cherrylakepublishing.com

Reading Adviser: Beth Walker Gambro, MS Ed., Reading Consultant, Yorkville, IL
Book Design: Felicia Macheske

Photo Credits: © Kiev.Victor/Shutterstock.com, cover; © Potapov Alexander/Shutterstock, 1; © TUM2282/Shutterstock, 5; © Sylphe_7/iStock, 6; © KobchaiMa/Shutterstock, 8; © FairytaleDesign/iStock, 11; © Tomasz Kobiela/Shutterstock, 12; © Dr Morley Read/Shutterstock, 15; © Tereshchenko Dmitry, 17; © fortuna777/Shutterstock, 19

Graphic Elements Throughout: © denniro/Shutterstock; © Libellule/Shutterstock; © sociologas/Shutterstock; © paprika/Shutterstock; © ilolab/Shutterstock; © Bruce Rolff/Shutterstock

45th Parallel Press is an imprint of Cherry Lake Publishing.

Library of Congress Cataloging-in-Publication Data

Names: Loh-Hagan, Virginia, author.
Title: Discover dragons / Virginia Loh-Hagan.
Description: Ann Arbor, Michigan : Cherry Lake Publishing, [2023] | Series: Magic, myth, and mystery express | Audience: Grades 2-3 | Summary: "Do dragons only breathe fire? How long does it take for a baby dragon to hatch? Books in the Magic, Myth, and Mystery Express series for young readers explore spooky creatures that go bump in the night, fill our dreams (or nightmares!), and make us afraid of the dark. Written with a high-interest level to appeal to a more mature audience and a lower level of complexity, clear visuals help struggling readers along. Considerate text includes fascinating information and wild facts to hold readers' interest, and support comprehension. Includes table of contents, glossary with simplified pronunciations, and index"—Provided by publisher.
Identifiers: LCCN 2022039296 | ISBN 9781668919675 (hardcover) | ISBN 9781668920695 (paperback) | ISBN 9781668922026 (ebook) | ISBN 9781668923351 (pdf)
Subjects: LCSH: Dragons—Juvenile literature. | Animals, Mythical—Juvenile literature.
Classification: LCC GR830.D7 L5834 2023 | DDC 398.24/54—dc23/eng/20220826
LC record available at https://lccn.loc.gov/2022039296

Cherry Lake Publishing would like to acknowledge the work of the Partnership for 21st Century Learning, a network of Battelle for Kids. Please visit *http://www.battelleforkids.org/networks/p21* for more information.

Printed in the United States of America
Corporate Graphics

Dr. Virginia Loh-Hagan is an author, university professor, former classroom teacher, and curriculum designer. She loves dragons! She was born in the year of the dragon! She lives in San Diego with her very tall husband and very naughty dog-dragons.

CONTENTS

CHAPTER ONE

Fierce Fire Beasts

Dragons were here before people. They're magical beasts. They make fire!

They have giant lizard or snake bodies. They have large bat wings.

Dragons were first found on the eastern coast of Asia.

Western dragons come from Europe, North America, and South America. They're powerful. They're also evil. They're greedy. They **hoard** treasure. Hoard means to store and not share.

Dragons live all over the world.

Explained by
SCIENCE

Dragons shouldn't be able to fly. It doesn't make sense. They are too heavy. Their wings are too small.

Eastern dragons come from Asia. They're smaller. They don't have wings.

They're good. They're lucky. They fight evil.

Chinese dragons control the rain, rivers, lakes, and sea.

Know the LINGO!

Basilisk: a large snake-dragon that can kill people by looking at them

Knuckers: dragons that can't fly

Lair: a dragon's home

CHAPTER TWO

Beware of the Beasts!

Dragons are strong. They make fire. They make **acid**. Acid is a chemical substance that can burn things.

They make ice. They breathe out the fire, acid, and ice. Their breath can kill.

It looks like dragons are breathing fire, but they're making it in their mouths.

Dragon blood has power. It comes from dead dragons. Evil dragon blood has poison. One drop can kill a person. Good dragon blood can heal.

Dragon blood can make human skin invincible. This means it can't be harmed.

Did You KNOW?

People thought rain clouds were dragon breath. They thought thunder was dragon breath. They thought lightning was dragon breath.

Have You HEARD?

Komodo dragons are lizards. They live in Indonesia. They look like dragons. They're the world's biggest lizards. They're 10 feet (3 meters) long. They weigh 200 pounds (91 kilograms).

Dragons have super senses. They hear well. They smell well. They see really well. They have cat eyes. They have 3 eyelids. This protects their eyes when they fly.

Special eyelids protect dragon eyes from wind and weather.

CHAPTER THREE

Dragon-Slaying

Dragons have weaknesses. They don't live forever. But they live a long time. They live for thousands of years.

There are many stories about heroes and knights slaying dragons.

STAY SAFE!

- Don't wear jewelry! Dragons want jewels. They will kill you to get them.

- Don't listen to a dragon. They like to trick people.

Their heads can be chopped off. This stops dragons from breathing fire. Dragons are magical. Magic can stop them. But it can't kill them.

Any creature that eats a dragon egg will become a dragon.

CHAPTER FOUR

From Eggs to Beasts

Dragons start out as eggs. The eggs are the same color as the mother dragon. They take years to hatch. **Hatchlings** are baby dragons. Hatchlings have soft scales. Their scales are like feathers. The scales slowly harden. Hatchlings are helpless.

ORIGINS

Herodotus lived in ancient Greece. He wrote about dragons in 450 BCE. He saw new animals that could fly. He saw large dragon bones.

Real WORLD

J. P. de Kam is like a human dragon. He breathes fire as his job. He is also a **BASE jumper**. This is a person who jumps from a high place and lands with a parachute. He did these things together. He breathed fire when he did a BASE jump.

CONSIDER THIS!

Say What?

Read the Magic, Myth, and Mystery Express book about mermaids. Think about how dragons and mermaids can both be bad and good. Explain how they are the same.

Think About It!

People used to think the world was flat. Dragons were said to be at the edge of the world. Pictures of dragons were normal on early maps. They marked new places. They were warnings. Why would people be afraid of these places?

LEARN MORE

Caldwell, S. A. *The Magnificent Book of Dragons*. San Rafael, CA: Weldon Owen International, 2021.

Drake, Ernest. *Dragonology: The Complete Book of Dragons*. Cambridge, MA: Candlewick, 2021.

Macfarlane, Tamara, and Alessandra Fusi. *Dragon World*. New York: DK, 2021.

Seraphini, Temisa, and Sophie Robin. *The Secret Lives of Unicorns*. London; New York: Flying Eye Books, 2019.

Glossary

acid (A-suhd) a chemical substance the can burn things

BASE jumper (BAYS JUHM-puhr) a person who jumps from a high place and lands with a parachute

Eastern (EE-stuhrn) from the eastern part of the world, such as Asia

hatchlings (HACH-lings) baby dragons

hoard (HOHRD) to collect and store things without sharing

Western (WEH-stuhrn) from the western part of the world, such as Europe and North and South America

Index